PASTA
COOKING

® Landoll, Inc.
Ashland, Ohio 44805
Text and photographs
© 1995 Coombe Books Ltd.
Cover
© 1996 Landoll, Inc.

Photography by Peter Barry
Recipes by Judith Ferguson, Patricia Payne and Fréderic Lebain
Designed by Richard Hawke
Edited by Jillian Stewart

3260
© 1993 Coombe Books
This edition published 1995 by Landoll, Inc. Ashland, Ohio
44805. No part of this book may be reproduced or copied.
All rights reserved. Manufactured in the U.S.A.
ISBN 1-56987-437-9

PASTA

COOKING

® Landoll, Inc.
Ashland, Ohio 44805

Contents

Introduction

Pasta has become increasingly popular over the last few years. Pasta is literally a paste made with flour and eggs. Commercial pasta is usually made from hard durum wheat, but fresh pasta can be made with almost any kind of flour. It can also be made in a variety of different colors with the addition of ingredients such as spinach and tomato paste.

You can make pasta at home, but it is often more convenient to buy the fresh varieties now available in supermarkets. A wide range of dried, packaged pastas are also on offer, but these do not match the taste of the real thing! Pasta comes in a bewildering array of names and shapes. Because the Italian names often vary depending on which region the pasta originates from, it is often easier to look for the shape of the particular pasta you require.

Pasta is the perfect complement to a wide range of other ingredients. It can simply be mixed with olive oil and garlic or fresh herbs, or it can be enhanced with everything from tomatoes and cheese to ham and olives. Tomatoes, cheese and herbs are the most common ingredients in pasta sauces and fillings, but even within these categories there are numerous flavors and uses. Parmesan is treasured for its wonderful flavor, while ricotta is perfect for stuffing pasta as it adds body and holds its shape well. One of the joys of cooking pasta is that it combines so well with numerous ingredients, so experiment with your favorites to find flavors that you enjoy.

One of the bonuses of pasta is that it is simple and quick to cook, but a few guidelines should be followed. Never overcook pasta as it will quickly become sticky. Remember that fresh pasta cooks more quickly than the dried variety. Whole wheat pasta takes longer to cook and cooking times will also vary according to the thickness of the pasta. Most important, pasta should be cooked in a large, uncovered saucepan of boiling, salted water. A little olive oil can be added to prevent the pasta sticking, and the water boiling over.

The ease of cooking and variety of shapes and flavors ensures that pasta is here to stay, so start experimenting with some of the recipes in this book, and you will find that producing the perfect pasta dish is simplicity itself.

MEATBALL SOUP

*A filling soup which makes a meal
in itself when served with bread.*

SERVES 4

1 lb beef bones (see Cook's Tip)
1 carrot
1 onion, chopped
1 celery stalk, chopped
1 egg, beaten
½ lb ground beef
½ cup bread crumbs
Salt and pepper
1 tbsp oil
14 oz can crushed plum tomatoes
¾ cup small pasta
1 tbsp chopped fresh parsley

1. Place bones, carrot, onion and celery in a large saucepan and cover with cold water. Bring to a boil, cover and simmer for at least one hour.

2. Meanwhile, mix lightly beaten egg with ground beef, bread crumbs and plenty of seasoning.

3. Take a teaspoon of the mixture and roll into small balls. Heat oil in a roasting pan and put in the balls. Bake in a preheated oven at 350°F for 45 minutes, turning occasionally.

4. Strain stock into a saucepan.

5. Add tomatoes to stock. Bring to a boil, and simmer for 15 minutes. Add pasta and cook for 10 minutes, stirring frequently.

6. Add meatballs, adjust seasoning, and stir in chopped parsley. Serve hot.

TIME: Preparation takes 10 minutes, cooking takes 1 hour 40 minutes.

COOK'S TIP: Use a beef stock cube instead of the beef bones. Dissolve the stock cube in a little boiling water, add to the saucepan with the vegetables and cover with cold water.

MINESTRA

*Some of Italy's finest ingredients
make up this warming soup.*

SERVES 4

---

1 onion
1 carrot
1 celery stalk
2 tbsps olive oil
6 cups water
Salt and pepper
½ lb fresh spinach
2 tomatoes
4 oz elbow macaroni
2 cloves garlic, crushed
2 tbsps chopped fresh parsley
1 tsp fresh rosemary or ½ tsp dried
¼ cup Parmesan cheese, grated

---

1. Cut onion, carrot and celery into thick, julienne.

2. Heat oil in a large, heavy pan and fry vegetable strips until just brown, stirring occasionally. Pour on water, season with salt and pepper, and simmer for 20 minutes.

3. Meanwhile, wash and cut spinach leaves into shreds, add to soup and simmer for 10 minutes.

4. Blanch and peel tomatoes and chop coarsely, removing seeds.

5. Add tomatoes, macaroni, garlic, parsley and rosemary to the soup, and simmer another 10 minutes. Adjust seasoning. Serve with grated Parmesan cheese if desired.

TIME: Preparation takes 15 minutes, cooking takes 45 minutes.

MACARONI WITH OLIVE SAUCE

Macaroni is served here with butter, garlic and finely chopped olives.
A very tasty dish that makes an ideal appetizer.

SERVES 4

11 oz macaroni
¼ cup butter
1 clove garlic, finely chopped
10 pitted olives, green and/or black, finely
    chopped
Salt and pepper

1. Cook the macaroni to your liking in salted, boiling water. Rinse in hot water and set aside to drain.

2. Melt the butter in a saucepan and add the garlic and olives. Cook for 1 minute and then stir in the macaroni.

3. Check the seasoning, adding salt and pepper as necessary. Serve hot.

TIME: Preparation takes about 10 minutes, cooking takes approximately 20 minutes.

VARIATION: Add a few chopped capers to the olives, but reduce the amount of salt.

COOK'S TIP: Rinse the macaroni really well under hot water to prevent it from sticking together.

VERMICELLI PESCATORE

*This impressive dish is simple to prepare
and perfect for special guests.*

SERVES 4

12 mussels
12 clams
½ lb cod fillets
¼ lb squid, cleaned
4 large shrimp, cooked
4 fresh oysters, cooked
3 cups tomato sauce
¼ cup olive oil
1 cup dry white wine
Half a green pepper, diced
Salt and pepper
9 oz package vermicelli

1. Prepare seafood. If using fresh mussels, clean closed mussels, removing beard, and cook in boiling water for 3 minutes until they open. (Discard any that remain closed).

2. Cool and remove from shells, keeping a few in shells for garnish if desired. Cut cod into ½ inch pieces.

3. Cut squid into rings.

4. Heat 2 tbsps oil in a pan and add the squid. Fry gently until golden brown, then add wine, tomato sauce, green pepper, and salt and pepper to taste. Simmer for 20 minutes and then add cod. Simmer for another 10 minutes, stirring occasionally.

5. Add clams and mussels and bring mixture back to a boil; adjust seasoning. Meanwhile, cook vermicelli in plenty of boiling, salted water for 10 minutes, or until tender but still firm. Drain well. Add seafood mixture and toss. Garnish with shrimps and oysters.

TIME: Preparation takes 15 minutes, cooking takes 40 minutes.

CABBAGE AND PASTA SOUP

Chicken stock flavored with bacon, cabbage, pasta and garlic is the base for this light and tasty appetizer.

SERVES 4

6 leaves white cabbage
1 tbsp olive oil
5 oz small pasta shells
2 slices bacon
1 clove garlic, chopped
3 cups chicken stock
Salt and pepper

1. Cut the cabbage into thin strips. To do this, roll the leaves into cigar shapes and cut with a very sharp knife.

2. Heat the olive oil. Trim excess fat from bacon, dice meat and fry the bacon, garlic and cabbage together for 2 minutes.

3. Pour over the stock, season with salt and pepper and cook on a moderate heat for 15 minutes.

4. Add the pasta to the soup and cook for another 15 minutes.

5. Check the seasoning and serve.

TIME: Preparation takes about 5 minutes, cooking takes approximately 35 minutes.

SERVING IDEA: Sprinkle over a little grated Parmesan cheese just before serving the soup.

VARIATION: Leave the piece of bacon whole and remove before serving the soup.

CHICK PEA SOUP

*This unusual sounding soup is a wonderful mixture
of chick peas and classic Italian ingredients.*

SERVES 4

1 cup dried chick peas
3 tbsps olive oil
2 cloves garlic
1½ cups plum tomatoes, chopped
3 cups water
1 tsp fresh basil or ½ tsp dried
1 chicken bouillon cube
Salt and pepper
1 cup small pasta or elbow macaroni
2 tbsps Parmesan cheese, grated

1. Soak chick peas overnight in enough water to cover by 1 inch. Drain and discard water. Place the chick peas in a large, heavy pan, and cover with 1 inch of water. Bring to a boil and simmer, covered, for about 1 hour until chick peas are tender. Make sure they do not boil dry.

2. Heat olive oil in a heavy pan and sauté garlic cloves. When browned, remove and discard garlic cloves. Add tomatoes and their juice, water and basil, and simmer for 20 minutes.

3. Add drained chick peas, crumbled bouillon cube, and salt and pepper to taste. Stir well and simmer another 10 minutes. Bring back to a boil. Add pasta and cook, stirring frequently, for 10 minutes.

4. Mix in half of the Parmesan cheese. Adjust seasoning and serve immediately, with remaining Parmesan cheese sprinkled on top.

TIME: Preparation takes overnight soaking for the chick peas plus 5 minutes, cooking takes 1 hour 20 minutes.

COOK'S TIP: Soup may be puréed before pasta is added, if desired.

BEAN SOUP

*Kidney beans and pasta combine to produce
a filling soup suitable for all the family.*

SERVES 4-6

15 oz can kidney beans
2 slices bacon, chopped
1 celery stalk, chopped
1 small onion, chopped
1 clove garlic, crushed
½ cup plum tomatoes, chopped
   and seeds removed
1 tbsp chopped fresh parsley
1 tsp fresh basil or ½ tsp dried
4 cups water
1 chicken bouillon cube
Salt and pepper
1 cup whole wheat pasta

1. Place kidney beans, bacon, celery, onion, garlic, parsley, basil, tomatoes and water in a large saucepan. Bring to a boil and add bouillon cube and salt and pepper to taste. Cover and cook on a low heat for about 1½ hours.

2. Raise heat and add pasta, stirring well. Stir frequently until pasta is cooked but still firm – about 10 minutes. Serve immediately.

TIME: Preparation takes 15 minutes, cooking takes 1 hour 45 minutes.

MARINER'S SALAD

*Seafood mixes very well with pasta and the
ingredients can be adapted according to availability.*

SERVES 6

1 lb pasta shells, plain and spinach
4 large scallops, cleaned
1 cup mussels
½ cup lemon juice and water mixed
¾ cup cooked, peeled and de-veined
    shrimp
½ cup clams, cooked
4 oz cooked crab meat, diced
4 green onions, chopped
1 tbsp chopped fresh parsley

Dressing
Grated rind and juice of half a lemon
1 cup mayonnaise
2 tsps paprika
⅓ cup sour cream or plain yogurt
Salt and pepper

1. Cook the pasta for 10 minutes in a large pan of boiling, salted water with 1 tbsp oil. Drain and rinse under hot water. Leave in cold water until ready to use.

2. Cook the scallops and mussels in the lemon juice and water mixture for about 5 minutes, or until fairly firm.

3. Cut the scallops into 2 or 3 pieces, depending upon size.

4. Prepare the dressing and drain the pasta thoroughly.

5. Mix all ingredients together and coat completely with dressing. Stir carefully so that the shellfish do not break-up. Chill for up to 1 hour before serving.

TIME: Preparation takes 25 minutes, cooking takes 15 minutes.

CURRIED SHRIMP SALAD

*An unusual salad which is perfect
for a summer lunch.*

SERVES 4

2 tbsps olive oil
1 clove garlic, crushed
1 small onion, chopped
1½ tsps curry powder
1 tsp paprika
1 tsp tomato paste
½ cup water
2 slices lemon
Salt and pepper
1 tsp apricot preserve
1 cup mayonnaise
1½ cups small pasta or elbow macaroni
½ lb cooked shrimp, peeled and de-veined
Juice of ½ a lemon

1. Heat oil, and fry garlic and onion gently until soft but not colored. Add curry powder and paprika, and cook for 2 minutes.

2. Stir in tomato paste and water. Add lemon slices, and salt and pepper to taste. Cook slowly for 10 minutes.

3. Stir in the preserve, and bring to a boil, simmering for 2 minutes. Strain and leave to cool. Add mayonnaise.

4. Meanwhile, cook pasta in plenty of boiling salted water for 10 minutes, or until tender, but still firm. Rinse under cold water and drain well.

5. Toss in lemon juice, and put in serving dish. Arrange shrimp on top, and pour over curry sauce. Toss well. Sprinkle with paprika.

TIME: Preparation takes 10 minutes, cooking takes 20 minutes.

PASTA AND VEGETABLES IN PARMESAN DRESSING

Fresh vegetables and pasta in a delicious dressing.

SERVES 6

1 lb pasta spirals or other shapes
½ lb assorted vegetables such as:
Zucchini, cut in rounds or julienne
Broccoli, trimmed into very small florets
Snow peas, ends trimmed
Carrots, cut in rounds or julienne
Celery, cut in julienne
Cucumber, cut in julienne
Green onion, thinly shredded or sliced
Asparagus tips
Green beans, sliced
Red or yellow peppers, thinly sliced

Dressing
½ cup olive oil
3 tbsps lemon juice
1 tbsp sherry
1 tbsp fresh parsley, chopped
1 tbsp fresh basil, chopped, or ½ tbsp dried
¼ cup freshly grated Parmesan cheese
2 tbsps mild mustard
Salt and pepper
Pinch sugar

1. Cook pasta in a large saucepan of boiling, salted water with 1 tbsp oil for 10-12 minutes or until just tender. Rinse under hot water to remove starch. Leave in cold water.

2. Place all the vegetables except the cucumber into boiling salted water for 3 minutes until just tender. Rinse in cold water and leave to drain.

3. Mix the dressing ingredients together very well. Drain the pasta thoroughly and toss with the dressing. Add the vegetables and toss to coat. Refrigerate for up to 1 hour before serving.

TIME: Preparation takes 25 minutes, cooking takes 13-15 minutes.

Italian Pasta Salad

*Buy your favorite Italian cold cuts
for this delicious salad.*

SERVES 4-6

1 lb pasta shapes
½ cup frozen peas
8 oz assorted Italian cold cuts, cut in strips:
  salami, mortadella, prosciutto
4 oz provolone or mozzarella cheese, cut
  in strips
15 black olives, halved and pitted
4 tbsps capers
1 small red onion or 2 shallots, chopped
2 cups oyster mushrooms, stems trimmed
  and sliced

Dressing
3 tbsps white wine vinegar
½ cup olive oil
½ clove garlic, crushed
1 tsp fennel seed, crushed
1 tbsp fresh parsley, chopped
1 tbsp fresh basil, chopped, or ½ tsp dried
1 tbsp prepared mustard
Salt and pepper

1. Put the pasta in a large saucepan of boiling water with a pinch of salt and 1 tbsp oil. Cook for about 10 minutes or until just tender.

2. Add the frozen peas during the last 3 minutes of cooking. Drain the pasta and peas and rinse under hot water. Leave in cold water until ready to use.

3. Mix the dressing ingredients together well.

4. Drain the pasta and peas thoroughly. Mix the pasta and peas with the cold cuts and cheese, olives, capers, chopped onion or shallot and sliced mushrooms.

5. Pour the dressing over the salad and toss all the ingredients together to coat. Do not over-mix.

6. Leave the salad to chill for up to 1 hour before serving.

Time: Preparation takes 25 minutes, cooking takes 10 minutes.

Niçoise Salad

*A classic French salad using
Italy's favorite ingredients!*

SERVES 4

1½ cups penne

7 oz can tuna, drained and flaked

3 tomatoes, quartered

1 cucumber, cut into julienne

1 cup green beans, cooked

12 black olives, halved, with stones
    removed

6-8 anchovy fillets, drained, and soaked in
    milk if desired (see Cook's Tip)

½ cup oil and vinegar dressing

1. Cook penne in plenty of boiling, salted water until tender, but still firm.

2. Rinse in cold water, drain, and leave to dry.

3. Put flaked tuna in the bottom of a salad dish. Toss pasta with tomatoes, cucumber, green beans, olives, and anchovies, and then pour on dressing. Mix together well.

TIME: Preparation takes 15 minutes, cooking takes 15 minutes.

COOK'S TIP: Soaking the anchovy fillets in milk removes any excess salt
from the fish. Drain well before using.

TUNA AND TOMATO SALAD

*An economical salad which uses few
ingredients – perfect for unexpected guests.*

SERVES 4

---

1 tbsp chopped fresh basil or marjoram,
   or 1 tsp dried basil or oregano
6 tbsps vinaigrette dressing (see Cook's Tip)
3 cups pasta shells
7 oz can tuna, flaked
6 tomatoes

---

1. Mix herbs with vinaigrette dressing.

2. Cook pasta shells in a large saucepan of boiling salted water until tender – about 10 minutes. Rinse with cold water and drain, shaking off excess water. Toss with 3 tablespoons of vinaigrette dressing. Leave to cool.

3. Meanwhile, slice enough of the tomatoes to arrange around the outside of the serving dish.

4. Chop the rest, pour the remaining vinaigrette dressing over them, and place in the center of the dish.

5. Add tuna to the pasta shells, and toss gently. Serve in the center of the dish over the chopped tomatoes.

TIME: Preparation takes 10 minutes, cooking takes 15 minutes.

COOK'S TIP: To make your own vinaigrette dressing, mix 4½ tbsps olive oil with 1½ tbsps white wine vinegar, a pinch of salt and pepper and about ⅛-¼ tsp of prepared mustard.

MEXICAN CHICKEN SALAD

A simple salad which is both quick and tasty.

SERVES 4

1¼ cups pasta shells
2 cups cooked chicken, shredded
7 oz can corn, drained
1 celery stalk, sliced
1 red pepper, diced
1 green pepper, diced

Dressing
1 tbsp mayonnaise
2 tbsps vinegar
Salt and pepper

1. Cook pasta in plenty of boiling salted water until just tender. Drain well and leave to cool.

2. Meanwhile, combine mayonnaise with vinegar and salt and pepper to taste.

3. When the pasta has cooled, add chicken, corn, celery and peppers.

4. Toss together well and serve with the dressing.

TIME: Preparation takes 10 minutes, cooking takes 15 minutes.

GIANFOTTERE SALAD

*Eggplant, zucchini and peppers are
combined with pasta in this simple salad.*

SERVES 4

1 eggplant
2 tomatoes
1 zucchini
1 red pepper
1 green pepper
1 onion
4 tbsps olive oil
1 clove garlic
Salt and pepper
1 lb whole wheat pasta spirals or bows

1. Cut eggplant into ½ inch slices. Sprinkle with salt and set aside for 30 minutes.

2. Peel the tomatoes – put them into boiling water for 20 seconds, rinse in cold water, and peel the skins off. Chop coarsely.

3. Cut zucchini into ½ inch slices. Chop the peppers coarsely.

4. Chop the onion and garlic.

5. Heat 3 tbsps olive oil in pan and fry onion gently until transparent.

6. Meanwhile, rinse salt from eggplant, and pat dry with paper towels. Chop coarsely.

7. Add eggplant, zucchini, peppers, tomatoes and garlic to onion, and fry gently for 20 minutes. Season with salt and pepper. Allow to cool.

8. Meanwhile, cook pasta spirals in plenty of boiling, salted water for 10 minutes, or until tender but still firm. Rinse in cold water and drain well. Toss in the remaining 1 tbsp olive oil.

9. Toss vegetables together with pasta spirals.

TIME: Preparation takes 40 minutes, cooking takes 30 minutes.

ZUCCHINI SALAD

Raw vegetables are full of vitamins, and raw zucchini in particular
has the added advantage of having a delicious taste and texture.

SERVES 4

½ lb macaroni
4 tomatoes
4-5 zucchini, sliced thinly
8 stuffed green olives, sliced
6 tbsps vinaigrette dressing (see Cook's Tip)

1. Put the macaroni into a large saucepan and cover with boiling water. Add a little salt and simmer for 10 minutes, or until tender but still firm. Rinse in cold water and drain well.

2. Cut a small cross in the tops of each tomato and plunge into boiling water for 30 seconds.

3. Carefully remove the skins from the blanched tomatoes, using a sharp knife. Chop the tomatoes coarsely.

4. Mix all the ingredients in a large bowl and chill in the refrigerator for 30 minutes before serving.

TIME: Preparation takes 15 minutes, cooking takes about 10 minutes.

VARIATION: Use any other pasta shape of your choice.

COOK'S TIP: To make your own vinaigrette dressing, mix 4½ tbsps olive oil with 1½ tbsps white wine vinegar, a pinch of salt and pepper and about ⅛-¼ tsp of prepared mustard.

TUNA AND PASTA WITH RED KIDNEY BEANS

The perfect summer salad for lunch or a light dinner.

SERVES 4-6

1½ cups small pasta shells
8 oz can red kidney beans, drained
    and rinsed
1 cup small mushrooms, quartered
14 oz can tuna, drained and flaked
4 green onions, sliced
2 tbsps mixed fresh herbs chopped, or
    1 tbsp dried

Dressing
½ cup olive oil
3 tbsps white wine vinegar
Squeeze of lemon juice
1 tbsp Dijon mustard
Salt and pepper

1. Cook the pasta shells in boiling, salted
water with 1 tbsp oil for 10 minutes or
until just tender. Rinse under hot water
and then place in cold water until ready to
use.

2. Mix the dressing ingredients together
thoroughly.

3. Drain the pasta shells. Mix the pasta
with the beans, mushrooms, tuna, green
onions and herbs.

4. Pour over the dressing and toss to coat.
Chill up to 1 hour in the refrigerator
before serving.

TIME: Preparation takes 20 minutes, cooking takes 10 minutes.

SPAGHETTI AMATRICIANA

This is another quickly cooked sauce with a rich spicy taste.
Reduce the amount of chili pepper for a less fiery flavor.

SERVES 4

1 onion
6 slices Canadian bacon
1 lb ripe tomatoes
1 red chili pepper, diced
1½ tbsps oil
12 oz spaghetti
Parmesan cheese (optional)

1. Slice the onion thinly. Cut the bacon into thin strips.

2. Drop the tomatoes into boiling water for 6-8 seconds. Remove with a draining spoon, place in cold water, and leave to cool completely. This will make the skin easier to remove.

3. Peel the tomatoes, cut them in half and remove the seeds and pulp with a teaspoon. Rub the seeds and pulp through a strainer and retain juice to use in the sauce if desired. Chop the tomato flesh roughly and set it aside.

4. Heat the oil in a sauté pan and add the onion and bacon. Stir over medium heat for about 5 minutes, until the onion is transparent. Drain off excess fat, add the tomatoes and pepper, and mix well. Simmer the sauce gently, uncovered, for about 5 minutes, stirring occasionally.

5. Meanwhile, cook the spaghetti in boiling, salted water with 1 tbsp oil for about 10-12 minutes. Drain and rinse in hot water and toss in a colander to dry. To serve, spoon the sauce on top of the spaghetti and sprinkle with freshly grated Parmesan cheese, if desired.

TIME: Preparation takes about 20-25 minutes, cooking takes about 10-12 minutes for the spaghetti and about 8 minutes for the sauce.

Pasta Spirals with Creamy Parsley Sauce

Serve this quick and easy dish with French bread for the perfect mid-week dinner.

SERVES 3-4

2 tbsps butter or margarine
1 tbsp flour
1 cup milk
9 oz pasta spirals
1 tbsp chopped fresh parsley
1 tbsp lemon juice or 1 tsp vinegar

1. Heat butter in pan; when melted, stir in flour. Heat gently for 1 minute. Remove from heat, and gradually stir in milk. Return to heat, and stir continuously until boiling. Cook for 2 minutes.

2. Meanwhile, cook pasta spirals in plenty of boiling, salted water for 10 minutes, or until tender, but still firm. Rinse in hot water, and drain well.

3. Just before serving, add parsley and lemon juice to sauce, and pour over pasta. Serve immediately.

TIME: Preparation takes 5 minutes, cooking takes 15 minutes.

Tortiglioni alla Puttanesca

*Anchovy fillets add a special flavor
to this classic Italian dish.*

SERVES 4

7 oz can plum tomatoes, drained
6-8 anchovy fillets
10 oz tortiglioni (pasta spirals)
2 tbsps olive oil
2 cloves garlic, crushed
½ tsp fresh or pinch dried basil
Pinch chili powder
½ cup black olives, pitted and chopped
2 tbsps chopped fresh parsley
Salt and pepper

1. Chop tomatoes and anchovies.

2. Cook pasta in plenty of boiling salted water for 10 minutes, or until tender but still firm. Rinse in hot water and drain. Pour into a warmed bowl.

3. Meanwhile, heat oil in pan, add garlic, basil and chili powder, and cook for 1 minute.

4. Add tomatoes, olives, parsley and anchovies, and cook for a few minutes.

5. Season with salt and pepper. Pour sauce over pasta and mix together thoroughly. Serve immediately.

Time: Preparation takes 10 minutes, cooking takes 15 minutes.

PASTA SHELLS WITH MUSHROOM SAUCE

This adaptable dish can be served for lunch or dinner.

SERVES 3-4

½ lb mushrooms
2 tbsps butter or margarine
1 tbsp flour
1 cup milk
Salt and pepper
10 oz pasta shells

1. Rinse the mushrooms and chop them coarsely.

2. Melt butter in a saucepan and add mushrooms. Fry for 5 minutes, stirring occasionally. Stir in the flour and cook for 1 minute.

3. Reduce the heat, and add milk gradually, stirring continuously. Bring to a boil and cook for 3 minutes. Season with salt and pepper.

4. Meanwhile, cook the pasta shells in plenty of boiling salted water for 10 minutes, or until tender, but still firm.

5. Rinse in hot water and drain well. Place in a warmed serving dish, and pour over mushroom sauce. Serve immediately.

TIME: Preparation takes 5 minutes, cooking takes 15 minutes.

TAGLIATELLE WITH CREAMY LIVER SAUCE

Chicken livers are lovely mixed with cream and mushrooms;
add pasta to the mixture and you have the perfect mid-week treat.

SERVES 3-4

3 tbsps olive oil
2 medium onions, sliced
1 clove garlic, crushed
¾ cup mushrooms, sliced
1 lb chicken livers, cleaned and sliced
⅓ cup heavy cream
2 eggs, beaten
Salt and pepper
10 oz tagliatelle
1 tbsp chopped fresh parsley

1. Melt 2 tbsps of the oil in a large frying pan and cook onions and garlic gently until softened.

2. Add mushrooms and cook for 3 minutes. Add chicken livers, and cook until lightly browned. Remove from heat and stir in cream. Return to low heat and cook, uncovered, for another 2 minutes.

3. Remove from heat and stir in lightly beaten eggs. Season with salt and pepper to taste.

4. Meanwhile, cook the tagliatelle in plenty of boiling, salted water for 10 minutes, or until tender but still firm, stirring occasionally.

5. Drain tagliatelle, toss in remaining oil, and black pepper. Serve sauce over tagliatelle and sprinkle with parsley.

TIME: Preparation takes 10 minutes, cooking takes 15 minutes.

SPAGHETTI WITH TOMATO, SALAMI AND GREEN OLIVES

*Vary the quantities of salami and green olives
in this recipe according to your taste.*

SERVES 2-3

14 oz can plum tomatoes
⅓ lb salami, sliced and shredded
1 cup green olives, stoned and chopped
½ tbsp dried oregano
Salt and pepper
10 oz spaghetti
2 tbsps olive oil
1 clove garlic, crushed
¼ cup pecorino cheese, grated

1. Purée tomatoes in a blender or food processor and put into a saucepan. Add oregano, olives and salami and heat gently. Add salt and pepper to taste.

2. Meanwhile, cook spaghetti in plenty of boiling, salted water for 10 minutes, or until tender but still firm. Drain well.

3. Heat olive oil in the pan used to cook the spaghetti, and add garlic and freshly-ground black pepper.

4. Add spaghetti and pour the sauce over. Toss well. Serve immediately with pecorino cheese.

TIME: Preparation takes 15 minutes, cooking takes 15 minutes.

MACARONI CHEESE WITH HOT DOGS

Kids and adults alike will love this delicious, filling meal.

SERVES 4

8 hot dogs
1 lb macaroni
¼ cup butter or margarine
¾ cup all-purpose flour
2 cups milk
1½ cups cheddar cheese, grated
1 tsp dry mustard
Salt and pepper

Garnish
½ red pepper, cut into thin strips

1. Poach the hot dogs for 5-8 minutes. Remove skins and, when cold, cut into diagonal slices.

2. Cook macaroni in plenty of boiling salted water for about 10 minutes, or until tender but still firm. Rinse in hot water and drain well.

3. Meanwhile, melt the butter in a pan. Stir in the flour and cook gently for 1 minute. Reduce heat and gradually add milk, stirring all the time. Bring to a boil, stirring continuously, reduce heat and cook gently for 3 minutes.

4. Add hot dogs, grated cheese, mustard, and salt and pepper to taste. Stir well.

5. Add macaroni and mix in well. Pour mixture into an oven-proof dish and sprinkle the remaining cheese over the top.

6. Make a lattice of pepper, and cook under a preheated broiler until golden brown. Serve immediately.

TIME: Preparation takes 10 minutes, cooking takes 20 minutes.

Spirali with Spinach and Bacon

Pasta doesn't have to have a sauce that cooks for hours. This whole dish takes about 15 minutes. True Italian "fast food!"

SERVES 4

12 oz pasta spirals
8 oz fresh spinach
3 oz bacon
1 small red or green chili pepper
1 small red pepper
1 small onion
1 clove garlic, crushed
3 tbsps olive oil
Salt and pepper

1. Cook the pasta in boiling, salted water for about 10-12 minutes or until just tender. Drain the pasta in a colander and rinse it under hot water. Keep the pasta in a bowl of water until ready to use.

2. Tear the stalks off the spinach and wash the leaves well in the water several times. Set aside to drain.

3. Dice the bacon finely. Slice the chili and the red pepper finely. Slice the onion thinly.

4. Roll up several of the spinach leaves into a cigar shape and then shred them finely. Repeat until all the spinach is shredded.

5. Heat the oil in a sauté pan and add garlic, onion, peppers and bacon. Fry for 2 minutes, add the spinach and fry for another 2 minutes, stirring continuously. Season with salt and pepper.

6. Drain the pasta spirals and toss them in a colander to remove excess water. Mix with the spinach sauce and serve immediately.

TIME: Preparation takes 20 minutes, cooking takes about 15 minutes.

PENNE WITH HAM AND ASPARAGUS

*The Italian word penne means quills, due to the
diagonal cut on both ends.*

SERVES 4

8 oz penne
12 oz fresh asparagus
4 oz cooked ham
2 tbsps butter or margarine
1 cup heavy cream
Parmesan cheese (optional)

1. Trim asparagus spears about 1 inch from the bottom.

2. Cut the ham into strips about ½-inch thick.

3. Steam the asparagus spears for about 2 minutes. Drain and allow to cool.

4. Cut the asparagus into 1 inch lengths, leaving the tips whole.

5. Melt the butter in the sauté pan and add the asparagus and ham. Cook briefly to evaporate the liquid and then add the cream. Bring to a boil and cook for about 5 minutes to thicken the cream.

6. Meanwhile, cook the pasta in boiling salted water with 1 tbsp oil for about 10-12 minutes.

7. Drain the pasta and rinse under hot water. Toss in a colander to drain and mix with the sauce. Serve with grated Parmesan cheese, if desired.

TIME: Preparation takes about 20 minutes, cooking takes
10-12 minutes for the pasta and 8 minutes for the sauce.

HOMEMADE TAGLIATELLE WITH SUMMER SAUCE

Pasta making is not as difficult as you might think. It is well worth it, too, because homemade pasta is in a class by itself.

SERVES 4

Pasta Dough
1 cup all-purpose flour
1 cup bread flour
2 large eggs
2 tsps olive oil
Pinch salt

Sauce
1 lb unpeeled tomatoes, seeded and diced
1 large green pepper, diced
1 onion, diced
1 tbsp fresh basil, chopped, or ½ tsp dried
1 tbsp fresh parsley, chopped
2 cloves garlic, crushed
½ cup olive oil and vegetable oil, mixed

1. Combine all the sauce ingredients, mixing well. Cover and refrigerate overnight.

2. Place the flours in a mound on a work surface and make a well in the center. Place the eggs, oil and salt in the center of the well.

3. Using a fork, beat the ingredients in the center to blend them and gradually incorporate the flour from the outside edge. The dough may also be mixed in a food processor.

4. When half the flour is incorporated, start kneading using the palms of the hands until all the flour is incorporated. This may also be done in a food processor. Cover the dough and leave it to rest for 15 minutes.

5. Divide the dough in quarters and roll out thinly with a rolling pin on a floured surface, dusting dough lightly with flour before rolling. If using a pasta machine, following the manufacturer's directions. Allow the sheets of pasta to dry for about 10 minutes on a floured surface or tea towels. Cut the sheets into strips about ¼ inch wide by hand or machine, dusting lightly with flour while cutting. Leave the cut pasta to dry for 5-10 minutes.

6. Cook the pasta for 5-6 minutes in boiling, salted water with a spoonful of oil. Drain the pasta and rinse under very hot water. Toss in a colander to drain excess water. Place the hot pasta in serving dish. Pour the cold sauce over and toss well.

TIME: Preparation takes about 30 minutes, cooking takes about 5-6 minutes.

PASTA WITH FRESH TOMATO AND BASIL SAUCE

Pasta is a good addition to a healthy diet, as it is very filling and can be served with a variety of low calorie sauces.

SERVES 4-6

1 small onion, finely chopped
1 lb fresh tomatoes
2 tbsps tomato paste
1 orange
2 cloves garlic, crushed
Salt and freshly ground black pepper
½ cup red wine
½ cup chicken stock
2 tbsps coarsely chopped fresh basil
12 oz whole wheat pasta

1. Finely chop the onion.

2. Cut a small cross in the tops of the tomatoes and plunge them into boiling water for 30 seconds. Remove the tomatoes from the water and carefully peel away the loosened skin.

3. Cut the tomatoes into quarters, and remove and discard the seeds. Chop the tomato flesh coarsely, and put this, the onion and the tomato paste into a large saucepan.

4. Heat the onion and tomatoes over a gentle heat, stirring continuously until the tomatoes soften and begin to lose their juice.

5. Finely grate the orange rind. Cut the orange in half and squeeze out the juice.

6. Add the orange rind and juice to the large saucepan along with all the remaining ingredients except the pasta, and bring to a boil.

7. Continue to boil until the sauce has reduced and thickened, and the vegetables are soft.

8. While the sauce is cooking, put the pasta into another saucepan with enough boiling water to cover. Season with a little salt and cook for 10-15 minutes, or until the pasta is soft.

9. Drain the pasta in a colander and stir it into the hot sauce.

10. Serve at once with salad.

TIME: Preparation takes 15-20 minutes, cooking takes 10-15 minutes.

VARIATION: Add 1 cup thinly sliced mushrooms to the sauce.

LASAGNE WITH FOUR CHEESES

Adapt this dish by using your own
favorite Italian cheeses.

SERVES 2-3

1 tbsp olive oil
½ lb green lasagne
¼ cup butter
3 tbsps all-purpose flour
3¼ cups milk
6 tbsps grated Parmesan cheese
¼ cup grated gruyére cheese
¼ cup mozzarella, diced
¼ cup pecorino, diced
Salt, pepper and nutmeg

1. Fill a large pan with salted water. Add the olive oil. Cook the lasagne 4 or 5 sheets at a time for 7-10 minutes. Lift each batch out carefully and plunge into cold water. When all the pasta has been cooked, drain well on absorbent paper.

2. Melt the butter over gentle heat. When melted, add the flour and mix well. Heat the mixture gently until it turns a pale straw color. Stir in the milk gradually, stirring constantly until thick. Add the cheeses to the sauce, reserving 2 tbsps Parmesan. Season with salt, pepper and nutmeg.

3. Stir until the cheeses have melted.

4. Butter a deep baking dish generously. Add alternate layers of lasagne and sauce – there should be at least four layers. Finish with a layer of sauce, and sprinkle with the reserved grated Parmesan. Cook at 350°F for 45 minutes until bubbling and golden brown.

TIME: Preparation takes 15-20 minutes, cooking takes 45 minutes.

MEAT RAVIOLI WITH RED PEPPER SAUCE

Pepper-flavored pasta dough is rolled thinly, cut into squares, filled with a delicious meat stuffing and served with a creamy red pepper sauce.

SERVES 4

2 red peppers, seeded
1¾ cups all-purpose flour, sifted
2 eggs
1 cup ground beef
1 tbsp fresh parsley, finely chopped
½ onion, chopped
½ cup light cream
½ cup butter
Salt and pepper

1. Place the red peppers in a food processor and blend until liquid. Place in a small bowl and set aside, giving time for the pulp to rise to the surface. This takes approximately 30 minutes.

2. To make the dough, place the sifted flour in a bowl with a pinch of salt. Add 1 egg and 3 tbsps of the pepper pulp (not the juice).

3. Mix together really well and form into a ball. Set the dough aside for 30 minutes.

4. Mix together the meat, parsley and onion, and season with salt and pepper.

5. Roll the dough out very thinly, using a pasta machine if available, and cut into small squares. Place a little stuffing on half of the cut squares. Beat the remaining egg and brush the edges of the squares with the egg. Cover with another square of dough and seal the edges by pinching together with your fingers.

6. Bring a large saucepan of salted water to a boil and cook the ravioli for approximately 3 minutes – longer if you prefer your pasta well cooked.

7. While the ravioli are cooking, prepare the sauce by heating the cream with ½ cup of the red pepper pulp. Bring to a boil and then whisk in the butter.

8. Drain the ravioli and then pat them dry with a tea towel. Serve with the hot cream sauce.

TIME: Preparation takes about 50 minutes, resting time is 30 minutes and cooking time approximately 15 minutes.

VARIATION: Add a little wine vinegar (1 tsp) and a few drops of Tabasco to the sauce to give it a slightly peppery taste.

WATCHPOINT: When rolling out the dough, flour it well so that it does not stick to the rolling pin or pasta machine rollers.

SPAGHETTI WITH CRAB AND BACON

This recipe includes a wonderful preparation of home-made parsley pasta.
It is tossed and served with a seafood sauce, crab and bacon.

SERVES 4-6

1 bunch parsley (approximately 6 tbsps)
4¼ cups all-purpose flour
4 eggs
8 oz bacon
1 tbsp olive oil
¾ lb crab meat, chopped
1½ cups heavy cream
3 tbps butter
Fresh chervil, optional
Salt and pepper

1. Trim the leaves off the parsley, discard the stalks. Cook for 10 minutes in boiling water. Pass through a fine sieve and reserve the cooking liquid.

2. Purée the parsley with 3 tbsps of the cooking liquid in a blender.

3. In a bowl, mix together the flour, salt, eggs and 1½ tbsps parsley purée. Form into a ball.

4. Quarter the dough and form these pieces into balls. Press each ball flat and run it through a pasta machine, or roll out with a rolling pin.

5. Thin the dough progressively by passing it through the machine several times. Flour the dough frequently throughout the operation.

6. Run the flattened strips of dough through the spaghetti cutter or cut with a knife.

7. Cut the bacon first into strips and then into small rectangles.

8. Add the olive oil to boiling, salted water and cook the spaghetti for 5 minutes. Strain and rinse.

9. Break up the crab meat into small pieces with your fingers.

10. Heat the cream gently with the crab and bacon pieces.

11. Meanwhile, heat the butter in a pan and when it bubbles, add the spaghetti (first reheated by plunging for 30 seconds in boiling water). Mix well and season with salt and pepper.

12. Place the buttered spaghetti around the edges of the dinner plates and arrange the crab/bacon mixture in the center. Garnish with the fresh chervil.

TIME: Preparation takes 1 hour, cooking takes 20 minutes.

Cook's Tip: If you do not wish to prepare the spaghetti yourself you can buy fresh spaghetti, either parsley or plain verde, at a delicatessen or supermarket.

TAGLIATELLE WITH BLUE CHEESE

Fruit and cheese marries well to give a sweet and savory dish.

SERVES 6

4¼ cups all-purpose flour
5 eggs
1 tbsp olive oil
4 oz blue cheese (roquefort or stilton)
1 cup dried apricots
1¼ cups heavy cream
¼ cup milk
¼ cup pine nuts
½ bunch chives
Salt and pepper

1. In a bowl, work together the flour, a pinch of salt and eggs to form a soft ball of dough.

2. Quarter the dough and flatten each piece. Coat each piece with plenty of flour. Flour the rollers of a pasta machine and pass the dough through the machine, or roll it out with a rolling pin.

3. Continue rolling the pasta until thin. Flour frequently during the process.

4. Thread the dough strips through the tagliatelle cutter or cut into strips with a knife. Dredge the noodles with flour and allow to dry for 2 hours.

5. Bring to a boil a saucepan of salted water with 1 tbsp oil. Cook the pasta for 2 to 4 minutes, stirring with a fork.

6. Drain the tagliatelle and rinse in plenty of cold water to prevent sticking. Set aside.

7. Break up the cheese and force through a sieve with the back of a spoon.

8. Cut the apricots into strips, then dice.

9. Slowly heat the cream in a saucepan. Stir in the cheese and milk. Blend until smooth with a hand-held electric blender.

10. While the sauce is hot, stir in the tagliatelle and apricots, and season as necessary. Heat through quickly so the cream does not curdle or the noodles overcook.

11. Mix the pasta with two forks. Remove from the heat and mix in the pine nuts.

12. Chop the chives finely and sprinkle them over the tagliatelle; serve immediately.

TIME: Preparation takes 1 hour, cooking takes 16 minutes.
Drying the pasta takes 2 hours.

Pasta with Leeks and Mussels

*An easy pasta dish to prepare, ideal
for unexpected guests.*

SERVES 6

1 lb mussels
½ cup white wine
1 shallot, chopped
2 medium-sized leeks
¾ cup heavy cream
1 lb spiral-shaped pasta
1 tbsp oil
2 slices ham
1½ tbsps butter
Fresh chives to garnish
Salt and pepper

1. Scrub the mussels; remove the beards and wash in several changes of water to remove any sand.

2. In a large, covered saucepan, cook the mussels in the white wine with the chopped shallot for approximately 5 minutes, over a high heat.

3. Cool and remove the opened mussels from their shells. Reserve the cooking liquid.

4. Quarter each leek lengthwise, wash thoroughly and slice finely.

5. In a covered saucepan, cook the leeks in the cream, with salt and pepper to taste, for 10 minutes over a low heat.

6. In a large saucepan of boiling water, cook the pasta with 1 tbsp oil. Stir the pasta as it cooks, to prevent sticking.

7. Drain after 5 or 6 minutes. Rinse in cold water to prevent sticking.

8. Slice the ham into small pieces.

9. Strain the mussel cooking liquid through a sieve lined with cheesecloth. Measure out approximately ½ cup.

10. Add the shelled mussels and the mussel liquid to the cream mixture, and cook for 4 minutes, stirring constantly.

11. Melt the butter in a deep frying pan and reheat the pasta gently with the ham. Season to taste.

12. When the pasta is heated through, add the cream and leek sauce, and serve garnished with the chopped chives.

TIME: Preparation takes 30 minutes, cooking takes 25 minutes.

FISH RAVIOLI

This recipe has quite a few ingredients but it is not too difficult to prepare and the end result tastes wonderful.

SERVES 4

Dough
1¼ cups bread flour
Pinch of salt
3 eggs

Filling
½ lb sole or flounder fillets
1 slice of onion
1 slice of lemon
6 peppercorns
1 bay leaf
1 tbsp lemon juice
1 cup water
2 eggs, beaten
2 tbsps bread crumbs
1 green onion, finely chopped

Lemon sauce
2 tbsps butter or margarine
2 tbsps flour
1 cup strained cooking liquid from fish
2 tbsps heavy cream
2 tbsps lemon juice
Salt and pepper

Filling

1. Preheat oven to 350°F.

2. Wash and dry fish. Place in oven-proof dish with slice of onion, slice of lemon, peppercorns, bay leaf, lemon juice and water. Cover and cook for 20 minutes.

3. Remove fish from liquid and allow to drain. Strain liquid and set aside. When fish is cool, beat with the back of a spoon to a pulp.

4. Add eggs, bread crumbs and green onion, and salt and pepper to taste. Mix well.

Dough

1. Sift flour and salt into a bowl. Make a well in the center, and add the eggs. Work the flour and eggs together with a spoon, and then knead by hand until a smooth dough is formed. Leave to rest for 15 minutes.

2. Lightly flour a pastry board and roll out dough thinly into a rectangle. Cut dough in half.

3. Shape the filling into small balls and set them about 1½ inches apart on one half of the dough. Place the other half of the dough on top and cut with a ravioli cutter or small pastry cutter. Seal the edges.

4. Cook in batches in a large pan with plenty of boiling, salted water until tender – about 8 minutes. Remove carefully with a slotted spoon. Meanwhile, make sauce.

Sauce

1. Melt butter in a pan. Stir in flour and cook gently for 30 seconds. Reduce the heat and gradually stir in liquid from cooked fish. Return to heat and bring to a boil. Simmer for 4 minutes, stirring continuously.

2. Add cream and mix well. Season to taste. Remove from heat and gradually stir in lemon juice and seasoning. Do not reboil. Pour sauce over ravioli and serve immediately.

TIME: Preparation takes 30 minutes, cooking takes 30 minutes.

PASTITSIO

*This is like an Italian version of Shepherd's Pie
with macaroni instead of potato.*

SERVES 4

8 oz macaroni
4 tbsps butter or margarine
¼ cup Parmesan cheese, grated
Pinch of grated nutmeg
2 eggs, beaten
1 medium onion, chopped
1 clove garlic, crushed
1 lb ground beef
2 tbsps tomato paste
¼ cup red wine
½ cup beef stock
2 tbsps chopped fresh parsley
2 tbsps all-purpose flour
½ cup milk
Salt
Pepper

1. Preheat oven to 375°F.

2. Cook macaroni in plenty of boiling, salted water for 10 minutes, or until tender but still firm. Rinse under hot water. Drain.

3. Put one-third of the butter in the pan and return macaroni to it. Add half the cheese, nutmeg, and salt and pepper to taste. Leave to cool. Mix in half the beaten egg and put aside.

4. Melt half of the remaining butter in a pan and fry the onion and garlic gently until onion is soft. Increase temperature, add meat, and fry until browned.

5. Add tomato paste, stock, parsley and wine, and season with salt and pepper. Simmer for 20 minutes.

6. In a small pan, melt the rest of the butter. Stir in the flour and cook for 30 seconds. Remove from heat and stir in milk. Bring to a boil, stirring continuously, until the sauce thickens.

7. Beat in the remaining egg and season to taste. Spoon half the macaroni into a serving dish and cover with the meat sauce.

8. Put on another layer of macaroni and smooth over. Pour over white sauce, sprinkle with remaining cheese, and bake in the oven for 30 minutes until golden brown. Serve immediately.

TIME: Preparation takes 10 minutes, cooking takes 1 hour.

TORTELLINI

*Vary the amount of Parmesan cheese in
this recipe to suit your own taste.*

SERVES 4

Dough
1¼ cups bread flour
Pinch of salt
1 tbsp water
1 tbsp oil
3 eggs

Filling
2 tbsps cream cheese
1 cooked chicken breast, finely diced
2 tbsps ham, finely diced
2 spinach leaves, stalks removed, cooked
  and chopped finely
1 tbsp grated Parmesan cheese
1 egg, beaten
Salt and pepper

Sauce
1 cup heavy cream
¼ lb mushrooms, cleaned and sliced
¼ cup Parmesan cheese, grated
1 tbsp chopped fresh parsley
Salt and pepper

Filling

1. Beat the cream cheese until soft and smooth. Add chicken, ham, spinach and Parmesan cheese, and mix well. Add egg gradually, and salt and pepper to taste. Set aside.

Dough

1. Sift flour and salt onto a board. Make a well in the center. Mix water, oil and lightly beaten eggs together, and gradually pour into well, working in the flour with the other hand, a little at a time. Continue until the mixture comes together in a firm ball of dough.

2. Knead on a lightly-floured board for 5 minutes, or until smooth and elastic. Put into a bowl, cover with a cloth, and leave to stand for 15 minutes.

3. Roll dough out on a lightly-floured board as thinly as possible. Using a 2 inch cutter, cut out circles. Put ½ teaspoon of filling into the center of each circle. Fold in half, pressing edges together firmly. Wrap around forefinger, and press ends together. Cook in batches in a large pan, in plenty of boiling salted water for about 10 minutes until tender, stirring occasionally.

Sauce

1. Meanwhile, gently heat cream in a pan. Add mushrooms, Parmesan cheese, parsley, and salt and pepper to taste. Gently cook for 3 minutes.

To serve, toss sauce together with tortellini and sprinkle with parsley.

TIME: Preparation takes 30 minutes, cooking takes 15 minutes.

MEAT RAVIOLI

*Preparing your own pasta dough is very satisfying as it
almost always tastes better than packaged varieties.*

SERVES 4

Dough
1¼ cups bread flour
Pinch of salt
3 eggs

Filling
4 tbsps butter or margarine
1 clove garlic, crushed
1 onion, grated
½ lb ground beef
½ cup red wine
Salt and pepper
2 tbsps bread crumbs
½ cup cooked spinach, chopped
2 eggs, beaten

Sauce
14 oz can plum tomatoes
1 small onion, grated
1 small carrot, diced finely
1 bay leaf
3 parsley stalks
Salt and pepper
½ cup Parmesan cheese, grated

Filling
1. Heat butter in a frying pan. Add garlic
and onion, and fry gently for 1 minute.
Add ground beef and fry until browned.
Add red wine, and salt and pepper to
taste, and cook, uncovered, for 15 minutes.

2. Strain juices and reserve them for the
sauce. Allow to cool.

3. Add bread crumbs, chopped spinach,
and beaten eggs to bind.

4. Adjust salt and pepper to taste.

Dough
1. Sift flour in a bowl with salt. Make a
well in the center and add the eggs. Work
flour and eggs together with a spoon, then
knead by hand, until a smooth dough is
formed. Leave dough to rest for 15 minutes.

2. Lightly flour board, and roll out dough
thinly into a rectangle. Cut dough in half.

3. Shape the filling into small balls, and
set them about 1½ inches apart on one
half of the dough.

4. Place the other half of dough on top
and cut with a ravioli cutter or small
pastry cutter. Seal the edges by pinching
together or pressing with a fork.

5. Cook in batches in a large, wide pan
with plenty of boiling, salted water until
tender – about 8 minutes. Remove
carefully with a slotted spoon. Meanwhile,
make the sauce.

Sauce
1. Put all the sauce ingredients in a
saucepan. Add juice from cooked meat
and bring to a boil. Simmer for 10
minutes. Push through a sieve, and return
smooth sauce to pan. Adjust seasoning.

To serve, put ravioli in a warm dish and
cover with tomato sauce. Serve immediately,
sprinkled with grated Parmesan cheese.

TIME: Preparation takes 30 minutes, cooking takes 5 minutes.

FETTUCINE ESCARGOTS WITH LEEKS AND SUN-DRIED TOMATOES

These dried tomatoes keep for a long time and allow you to add a sunny taste to dishes whatever the time of year.

SERVES 4-6

6 sun-dried tomatoes
14 oz can escargots (snails), drained
12 oz fresh or dried whole wheat fettucine
3 tbsps olive oil
2 cloves garlic, crushed
1 large or 2 small leeks, trimmed, split,
   well washed and finely sliced
6 oyster, shittake or other large mushrooms
4 tbsps chicken or vegetable stock
3 tbsps dry white wine
6 tbsps heavy cream
2 tsps fresh basil, chopped
2 tsps fresh parsley, chopped
Salt and pepper

1. Drain the escargots well and dry with paper towels.

2. Place the fettucine in boiling salted water and cook for about 10-12 minutes, or until al dente. Drain, rinse under hot water and leave in a colander to drain dry.

3. Meanwhile, heat the olive oil in a frying pan and add the garlic and leeks. Cook slowly to soften slightly. Add the mushrooms and cook until the leeks are tender crisp. Remove to a plate. Add the drained escargots to the pan and cook over high heat for about 2 minutes, stirring constantly.

4. Pour on the stock and wine and bring to a boil. Boil to reduce by about a quarter and add the cream and tomatoes. Bring to a boil then cook slowly for about 3 minutes. Add the herbs, and salt and pepper to taste.

5. Add the leeks, mushrooms and fettucine to the pan and heat through. Serve immediately.

TIME: Preparation takes about 15-20 minutes.

LASAGNE NAPOLETANA

*This is a lasagne as it is cooked and eaten in Naples.
With its layer of red, green and white it looks as delicious
as it tastes and is very easy to prepare.*

SERVES 6

9 sheets spinach lasagne pasta
1 tbsp olive oil

Tomato Sauce

2 tbsps olive oil
2 cloves garlic, crushed
2 lbs fresh tomatoes, peeled, or canned
    tomatoes, drained
2 tbsps fresh basil, chopped, or 1 tbsp
    dried
Salt and pepper
Pinch sugar
6 whole basil leaves to garnish

Cheese filling

1 lb ricotta cheese
4 tbsps unsalted butter
2 cups Mozzarella cheese, grated
Salt and pepper
Pinch nutmeg

1. Cook the pasta for 8 minutes in boiling salted water with 1 tbsp oil. Drain and rinse under hot water and place in a single layer on a damp cloth. Cover with another damp cloth and set aside.

2. To prepare the sauce, cook the garlic in oil for about 1 minute in a large saucepan. When pale brown, add the tomatoes, basil, salt, pepper and sugar. (If using fresh tomatoes, drop into boiling water for 6-8 seconds. Transfer to cold water and leave to cool completely. This will make the skin easier to remove.)

3. Lower the heat and simmer the sauce for 35 minutes. Add more seasoning or sugar to taste.

4. Beat the ricotta cheese and butter together until creamy and stir into the remaining filling ingredients.

5. To assemble the lasagne, oil a rectangular baking dish and place 3 sheets of lasagne on the base. Cover with one third of the sauce and carefully spread on a layer of cheese. Place another 3 layers of pasta over the cheese and cover with another third of the sauce. Add the remaining cheese filling and cover with the remaining pasta. Spoon the remaining sauce on top.

6. Cover with foil and bake for 20 minutes at 375°F. Uncover and cook for 10 minutes longer. Garnish with the fresh basil leaves (if available) and leave to stand for 10-15 minutes before serving.

TIME: Preparation takes about 25 minutes, cooking takes about 1-1¼ hours.

ITALIAN CASSEROLE

*Serve this hearty main course with a
green salad or broccoli, and fresh bread.*

SERVES 4

1 cup small macaroni
2 tbsps butter or margarine
1 clove garlic, crushed
1 onion, chopped
2 16 oz cans plum tomatoes
1 tbsp tomato paste
1 red pepper, chopped coarsely
1 green pepper, chopped coarsely
½ lb salami, cut into chunks
10 pitted black olives, halved
½ lb mozzarella cheese, sliced thinly
Salt and pepper

1. Cook the macaroni in plenty of boiling salted water for 10 minutes, or until tender but still firm. Rinse under hot water and drain well. Place in a shallow, oven-proof dish.

2. Meanwhile, heat butter in pan, and fry onion and garlic gently until soft.

3. Add undrained tomatoes, tomato paste, red and green peppers, salami and olives, and stir well. Simmer uncovered for 5 minutes. Season with salt and pepper.

4. Pour over the macaroni, stir, and cover with the sliced cheese. Bake, uncovered, in a moderate oven at 350°F for 20 minutes, until cheese has melted. Serve immediately.

TIME: Preparation takes 15 minutes, cooking takes 40 minutes.

SPINACH LASAGNE

*Everyone will be asking for seconds when
they taste this delicious lasagne.*

SERVES 4

8 sheets green lasagne pasta

Spinach sauce
4 tbsps butter or margarine
3 tbsps flour
½ cup milk
1½ cups frozen spinach, thawed and
    chopped finely
Pinch of ground nutmeg
Salt
Pepper

Mornay sauce
2 tbsps butter or margarine
2 tbsps flour
1 cup milk
⅓ cup Parmesan cheese, grated
1 tsp Dijon mustard
Salt

1. To make spinach sauce, heat butter in pan, stir in flour and cook gently for 30 seconds.

2. Remove from heat and stir in milk gradually. Return to heat and bring to a boil, stirring continuously. Cook for 3 minutes.

3. Add spinach, nutmeg, and salt and pepper to taste. Set aside.

4. Cook spinach lasagne in lots of boiling salted water for 10 minutes, or until tender. Rinse in cold water, and drain carefully. Dry on a clean cloth.

5. To make mornay sauce, heat butter in a saucepan and stir in flour, cooking for 30 seconds.

6. Remove from heat and stir in milk. Return to heat, stirring continuously, until boiling. Continue stirring and simmer for 3 minutes.

7. Remove from heat and add mustard and two-thirds of cheese, and salt to taste.

8. Preheat oven to 400°F. Grease an oven-proof baking dish. Line the bottom with a layer of lasagne, followed by some of the spinach mixture and a layer of the cheese sauce. Repeat the process, finishing with a layer of lasagne and a covering of cheese sauce.

9. Sprinkle with the remaining cheese. Bake in a hot oven until golden on top. Serve immediately.

TIME: Preparation takes 10 minutes, cooking takes 30 minutes.

VANILLA CREAM MELBA

Elbow macaroni is enhanced with a delicious raspberry sauce and peaches in this easy-to-prepare dessert.

SERVES 4

⅔ cup small pasta or elbow macaroni
1½ cups milk
2½ tsps brown sugar
Few drops vanilla extract
½ cup heavy cream, lightly whipped
16 oz can peach halves
1 tsp cinnamon

Melba sauce
1 cup raspberries
2 tbsps confectioners sugar

1. Cook pasta in milk and sugar until soft. Stir regularly, being careful not to allow it to boil over. Remove from heat and stir in vanilla extract.

2. Pour pasta into a bowl to cool. When cool, fold in cream. Chill.

3. Meanwhile, make melba sauce. Push raspberries through a sieve, or purée in a blender or food processor. Mix in confectioners sugar to desired thickness and taste.

4. Serve pasta with peach halves and melba sauce. Dust with cinnamon if desired.

TIME: Preparation takes 15 minutes, cooking takes 10 minutes.

Black Cherry Ravioli with Sour Cream Sauce

A simple dough is mixed with cherries and cream to make the perfect ending to a meal.

SERVES 4

Dough
1¾ cups bread flour
1 tbsp sugar
3 eggs, lightly beaten

Large can pitted black cherries
¼ cup sugar
1 tsp cornstarch
½ cup sour cream
½ cup heavy cream

1. Put cherries in a sieve. Strain off the juice and reserve.

2. Make the dough by sifting flour and sugar in a bowl. Make a well in the center and add lightly-beaten eggs. Work flour and eggs together with a spoon, and then by hand, until a smooth dough is formed. Knead gently.

3. Lightly flour board, and roll dough out thinly into a rectangle. Cut dough in half. Put well-drained cherries about 1½ inches apart on the dough.

4. Place the other half on top and cut with a small glass or pastry cutter. Seal well around edges with back of a fork.

5. Boil plenty of water in a large saucepan, and drop in cherry pasta. Cook for about 10 minutes, or until they rise to the surface. Remove with a slotted spoon and keep warm. Keep 2 tablespoons cherry juice aside.

6. Mix 1 tablespoon cherry juice with cornstarch; mix remaining juice with sugar, put in small saucepan and set over heat. Add cornstarch mixture, and heat until it thickens.

7. Meanwhile mix sour cream and heavy cream together, and marble 1 tablespoon of cherry juice through it.

8. Pour hot, thickened cherry juice over cherry ravioli. Serve hot with cream sauce.

TIME: Preparation takes 30 minutes, cooking takes 15 minutes.

CHOCOLATE CREAM HELÈNE

*Pears, cream and pasta combine perfectly
in this simply delicious dessert.*

SERVES 4

⅔ cup small pasta or elbow macaroni
1½ cups milk
2½ tbsps sugar
1 tsp cocoa
½ cup heavy cream, lightly whipped
1 tbsp hot water
16 oz can pear halves

Garnish
Chocolate, grated

---

1. Cook pasta in milk and sugar until soft. Stir regularly, being careful not to allow it to boil over. Remove from heat.

2. Meanwhile, dissolve cocoa in hot water, and stir into pasta.

3. Pour pasta into a bowl to cool. When cool, fold in lightly-whipped cream. Chill. Serve with pear halves and a sprinkling of grated chocolate.

TIME: Preparation takes 15 minutes, cooking takes 10 minutes.

Index